Langston Hughes

Harlem Renaissance Writer

Dr. David H. Anthony and Stephanie Kuligowski, M.A.T.

Consultant

Marcus McArthur, Ph.D.
Department of History
Saint Louis Univeristy

Publishing Credits

Dona Herweck Rice, *Editor-in-Chief*
Lee Aucoin, *Creative Director*
Chris McIntyre, M.A.Ed., *Editorial Director*
Torrey Maloof, *Associate Editor*
Neri Garcia, *Senior Designer*
Stephanie Reid, *Photo Researcher*
Rachelle Cracchiolo, M.S.Ed., *Publisher*

Image Credits

cover The Granger Collection, New York; p.1 The Granger Collection, New York; p.4 The Granger Collection, New York; p. 5 The Granger Collection, New York; p.6 Yale Collection of American Literature, Beinecke Rare Book and Manuscript Library; p.7 (top) The Library of Congress; p.7 (bottom) Kansas State Historical Society; p.8 (left) The Library of Congress; p.8 (right) The Library of Congress; p.9 (top) from *Paul Laurence Dunbar: A Tribute*; archive.org; p.9 (bottom) Corbis; p.10 (top) The Library of Congress; p.10 (bottom) The Granger Collection, New York; p.11 The Granger Collection, New York; p.12 Shutterstock, Inc.; p.13 (top) Corbis; p.13 (bottom) The Granger Collection, New York; p. 14 (top) The Granger Collection, New York; p.14 (bottom) Alamy; p.15 The Granger Collection, New York; p.16 The Library of Congress; p. 17 The Library of Congress; p.18 (top) National Archives; p.18 (middle) The Library of Congress; p.18 (bottom) Getty; p.19 The Library of Congress; p.20 The Library of Congress; p.21 (left) Yale Collection of American Literature, Beinecke Rare Book and Manuscript Library; p.21 (right) Shutterstock, Inc.; p.22 (left) The Library of Congress; p.22 (right) The Granger Collection, New York; p.22 (bottom) Corbis; p.23 The Granger Collection, New York; p.24 Getty Images; p.25 (top) The Library of Congress; p.25 (bottom) The Library of Congress; p.26 (top) The Library of Congress; p.26 (bottom) The Library of Congress; p.27 The Library of Congress; p.29 (left) Getty Images; p.29 (top, right) Getty Images; p.29 (bottom, right) Getty Images; p.32 (left) The Granger Collection, New York; p.32 (right) National Archives

---

Teacher Created Materials
5301 Oceanus Drive
Huntington Beach, CA 92649-1030
http://www.tcmpub.com

ISBN 978-1-4333-1520-6

Table of Contents

Voice of a Generation

After the Civil War, **discrimination** made it hard for former slaves to start new lives. Unfair laws kept them at the bottom of Southern society. Many chose to flee the South. They headed north in search of freedom and jobs. This large movement of African Americans between 1865 and 1970 became known as the Great Migration.

Many of these **migrants** moved to New York City. They settled in a neighborhood called Harlem. There, African American culture flourished. Musicians, artists, and writers were inspired. They captured the excitement of the times in music, paint, and words. This period of creativity lasted from the end of World War I until the Great Depression. It is called the Harlem Renaissance. A **renaissance** is a new beginning.

Langston Hughes

Langston Hughes was a writer who lived in Harlem during this exciting time. From the center of African American life, he watched and wrote. He studied people on the streets. He listened to jazz music in clubs. He captured his world in words. In his poetry, plays, short stories, and autobiographies, he opened a window into African American culture. He is often called the voice of the Harlem Renaissance.

Harlem Renaissance painting, called *The Great Migration* by Jacob Lawrence.

The End of Slavery

During the Civil War, President Abraham Lincoln announced the Emancipation Proclamation. It freed the slaves in the Southern states. But it did not end slavery. When the war was over, the Thirteenth Amendment to the United States Constitution was written. This law finally ended slavery in the United States in 1865.

Separate Is Not Equal!

After the Civil War, Southern states passed laws to keep whites and African Americans separated. This was called **segregation** (seg-rih-GAY-shuhn). The laws were called **Jim Crow Laws**. African Americans were not allowed to go to the same schools as whites. They could not eat at the same restaurants as whites. Trains and buses had different seats for white and African American passengers. There were even separate pools and drinking fountains for whites and African Americans.

Growing Up

Respected Roots

James Mercer Langston Hughes was born in Joplin, Missouri, in 1902. His parents divorced, and his father moved to Mexico. His mother moved from place to place looking for jobs. So, Langston went to live with his grandmother, Mary, in Lawrence, Kansas.

Hughes's childhood was not easy. But his grandmother made him proud of his African **heritage**. She told him stories about his family. His great-uncle was John Mercer Langston. He was the first African American elected to the United States Congress from Virginia.

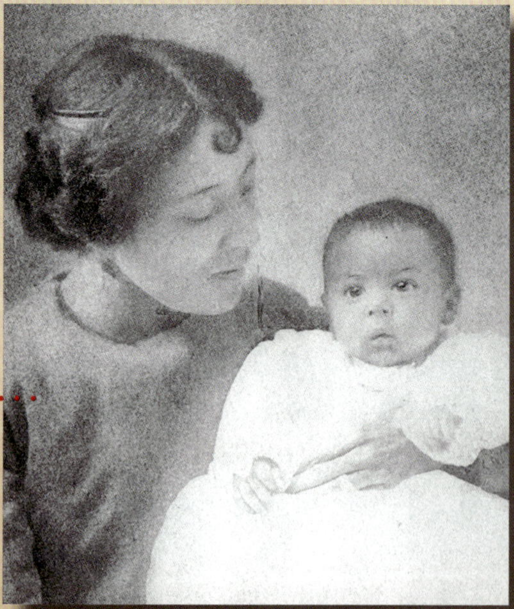

Langston and his mother

John Brown

John Brown was an **abolitionist**. He wanted to end slavery. He thought it was a sin. Brown believed violence was needed to end slavery. Some people agreed with Brown. Others thought he was wrong. When he stole weapons from the United States Army in Harpers Ferry, Virginia, he upset a lot of people. They thought he had committed a crime. But others thought Brown was a hero for what he did. When Brown was caught, he was put on trial. He was found guilty and hanged.

A Brave Past

Grandma Mary's second husband was Charles Henry Langston. This was Hughes's grandfather. He was an abolitionist, an educator, and an **activist** for African American rights.

John Brown's raid on Harpers Ferry

Lewis Sheridan Leary

Grandma Mary's first husband was another famous African American. He was Lewis Sheridan Leary. Leary fought with John Brown in the raid on Harpers Ferry. Brown, Leary, and others tried to take guns from the United States Army. They planned to give the guns to slaves so they could fight for their own freedom. The raid was unsuccessful. Leary was shot and killed. This event was one of the causes of the Civil War.

In 1910, President Theodore Roosevelt spoke at an event in Kansas. Grandma Mary sat on the platform as a special guest. Roosevelt honored her for her husband's role in the raid on Harpers Ferry. Hughes was proud of his family's heritage.

Discovering His Talent

As a teenager, Hughes went to live with his mother and stepfather in Lincoln, Illinois. He was a good student. He enjoyed reading and writing poetry.

Later, the family moved to Cleveland, Ohio, where Hughes went to high school. An English teacher introduced him to the poetry of Carl Sandburg and Walt Whitman. Hughes also liked the work of African American poet Paul Laurence Dunbar. All these poets used common, everyday language to express ideas. Hughes liked their style.

Teachers and classmates began to notice Hughes's writing talent. The school's **literary** magazine published many of his poems.

During the summer before his last year in high school, Hughes went to Mexico to visit his father. The two did not get along. His father wanted him to be an **engineer**. He wanted to be a writer.

Walt Whitman

Carl Sandburg

Hughes returned to Cleveland to finish high school. After graduation, he sent a poem to a magazine called *The Crisis*. The magazine published the poem. This showed Hughes's father that his son had real talent. He agreed to help pay for Hughes's college classes. In 1921, Hughes enrolled at Columbia University in New York City. The university was known for being one of the best in the country.

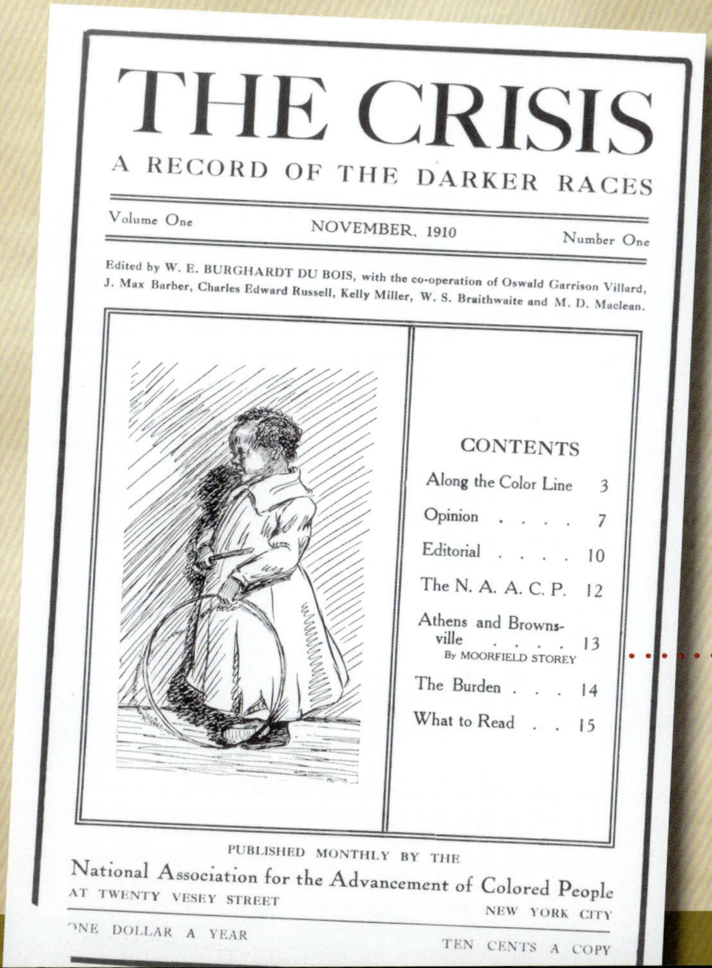

THE CRISIS

A RECORD OF THE DARKER RACES

Volume One NOVEMBER, 1910 Number One

Edited by W. E. BURGHARDT DU BOIS, with the co-operation of Oswald Garrison Villard, J. Max Barber, Charles Edward Russell, Kelly Miller, W. S. Braithwaite and M. D. Maclean.

CONTENTS

PUBLISHED MONTHLY BY THE
National Association for the Advancement of Colored People
AT TWENTY VESEY STREET NEW YORK CITY
ONE DOLLAR A YEAR TEN CENTS A COPY

The Crisis published by the NAACP

Paul Laurence Dunbar

Famous First

Paul Laurence Dunbar was the first African American poet to become famous. He also wrote novels and short stories. In his writings, he often discussed the problems that African Americans faced. Both African American and white readers recognized his talent.

Young Talent

The Crisis magazine published Hughes's poem, *"The Negro Speaks of Rivers."* Hughes wrote it at age 17 while crossing the Mississippi River on a train.

A Place to Call Home

While at college in New York, Hughes found his way to Harlem. Harlem had grown into a center of African American culture. Musicians, painters, and writers flocked there to live and create.

But artists were not the only people who lived in Harlem. African American activists moved there, too. The National Association for the Advancement of Colored People (NAACP) had its offices in the neighborhood. The NAACP works for African American **civil rights**.

Marcus Garvey

People United

Marcus Garvey started the Universal Negro Improvement Association (UNIA) to unite the African people who had been scattered by slavery. He wanted to bring them together to form a new nation. The government of the new nation would be run by and for these Africans. Garvey moved the UNIA to Harlem in the 1920s.

Fighting for Equality

The NAACP is still going strong. It has grown from 60 members in 1909 to more than 500,000 members.

Singer Billie Holiday (center) with musician friends

NAACP offices in Harlem

By the mid-1920s, more than half of the businesses in Harlem were owned by African Americans. African American musicians and singers starred in shows at the neighborhood's jazz clubs. African American magazines published the works of local writers and artists. Harlem was full of opportunities for African Americans.

Hughes found inspiration in Harlem. He spent lots of time in jazz clubs. He made friends with writers and artists. After a childhood spent moving, he had finally found a place where he belonged. Even though Hughes would travel and live in other places, he would always call Harlem home.

Life Lessons

College was not what Hughes expected. He faced racial discrimination while at Columbia University. He did not like the way he was treated. Hughes received good grades but he felt that the schoolwork took up too much of his time. He wanted to do more writing. He quit college after only one year.

Hughes took a job on a **freight** ship. A freight ship carries goods from place to place. While working aboard the ship, he traveled to many countries. In 1923, he visited the African countries of Senegal, Nigeria, Congo, Angola, Cameroon, and Guinea (GIN-ee). Not many African Americans back then had the chance to visit Africa. Africa made a big impression on Hughes.

Hughes traveled all over Africa. The red stars show the countries that he visited.

Hughes worked as a busboy at the Wardman Park Hotel in Washington, DC.

Dr. Carter G. Woodson

After his year at sea, Hughes moved to Washington, DC. He worked many different jobs. He sold newspaper ads, washed clothes, and made oyster stew. He also worked as an assistant to Carter G. Woodson. Woodson was a **historian**. He was the first person to study the history of African Americans.

Hughes wrote many poems during his short time in Washington, DC. One of these poems won first prize in a national poetry contest. Hughes also sold his first book of poems to a **publisher**.

The Father of Black History

In 1926, Woodson chose the second week in February as *Negro History Week*. This later became known as Black History Month, which is still celebrated today. It is said that Woodson chose February because President Lincoln was born on February 12. Lincoln issued the Emancipation Proclamation, helped the North win the Civil War, and worked to get the Thirteenth Amendment added to the United States Constitution. February is also believed to be the month of Frederick Douglass's birth. Douglass was a famous abolitionist. This may have been another reason Woodson chose this month.

Dr. Woodson

Woodson became Doctor Woodson in 1912. That year, he became the second African American to earn a Ph.D. from Harvard University. W. E. B. Du Bois was the first to do so in 1895.

Cotton Club

There were many nightclubs in Harlem. One of the most famous was the Cotton Club. Many African American musicians and singers performed there. But this club was segregated. African Americans were allowed to perform on stage, but they were not allowed to be in the audience.

Bebop

Young musicians also wanted to go to Harlem. In addition to the large orchestras in the 1920s and 1930s, there were smaller groups of musicians getting together. These smaller groups started to play music their own way. They called it *bebop*, and it changed jazz music forever.

The Cotton Club in Harlem was a popular place to hear jazz music.

Bebop pioneer Charlie "Bird" Parker (center) and his band

New Inspiration

Blues and Jazz

In the 1920s, Americans were excited about new types of music. These new sounds came from Southerners who had moved to northern cities. They were the sounds of blues and **jazz**.

Blues music came from slave work songs. It has a rhythm like a heartbeat. Blues songs also follow a pattern. Each **stanza** has three lines. The second line repeats the first line, and the third line rhymes with the others.

Jazz was created by African Americans in New Orleans, Louisiana. It mixed the sounds of African and European music. In the early days, jazz was played by big brass bands with trumpets, trombones, and saxophones. Later, pianos, guitars, and other instruments were added.

Musicians began playing blues and jazz in northern clubs. These clubs became popular with African Americans and whites. Hughes spent many evenings in jazz clubs. He loved the music. He thought it was an important part of African American culture. Hughes believed that blues and jazz music inspired African Americans to keep moving forward.

Duke Ellington and his orchestra

Musical Poetry

In 1926, Hughes published his first book of poetry. It was called *The Weary Blues*. Many of the poems in the book sounded like the music Hughes loved. Hughes used the rhyme patterns, rhythm, and repetition of blues and jazz music in his poems. This style became known as **jazz poetry**.

The next year, Hughes published his second book of poetry. Hughes wrote about the lives of ordinary African Americans. He celebrated African American culture.

During this time, Hughes returned to college. He enrolled at Lincoln University in Pennsylvania. This was the first African American college in the nation. He graduated in 1929. He was already on his way to becoming a famous writer.

Hughes attended Lincoln University in Pennsylvania.

1749 S St., N.W.,
Washington, D.C.,
October 29, 1925.

Mr. Walter White,
69 Fifth Avenue,
New York City.

Dear friend,

I am sorry I didn't get to see you last Sunday when you were here in Washington, but I am working in a hotel and my hours are such that I couldn't get away. I am trying to get the funds for college (Lincoln) in February but I'm afraid I won't make it without help so I've just written Mr. Johnson to see if he and The Garland Fund can't help me. What I want is this: A loan of about three hundred fifty dollars a year for the next three years, said money to be returned to the lender within three years after graduation. That would put me thru school. Some big hearted person ought to be interested enough in the developement of talent to grant me that.

My book of poems has gone to press. Now I'm working on my first book of prose which will perhaps be called Scarlet Flowers: The Autobiography of a Young Negro Poet. You think that's a good title? When will your new novel be published? People down here are waiting for it.

I haven't forgotten the very pleasant two hours spent with you, Mrs. White, and the little girl that Sunday morning in New York and I hope to see you again when I come up there. I Haven't ceased marvelling over the kid yet.

I hope we come out all right in Detroit. Getting Darrow is certainly fine. All good wishes to you,

Sincerely yours,

Langston Hughes

Hughes wrote a letter to the NAACP to ask for money to attend college at Lincoln University.

Earning fame did not mean that Hughes earned a lot of money. At that time, there had never been an African American writer who made a living by writing. Writers and other artists needed **patrons** (PEY-truhnz). Patrons are people who give artists money so they can make art. Hughes had patrons who supported him until he could support himself. Later in his life, Hughes became the first African American writer to support himself with his writing.

Harmon Awards

The Harlem Renaissance needed to find **philanthropists** (fi-LAN-throw-pists) to survive. A philanthropist is someone who donates something, often money, to someone in need. Artists needed to pay bills, but they were not making enough money from their art to pay them. In 1922, William E. Harmon started a foundation, or organization, to help give money to African American artists.

And the Winner Is...

The Harmon Foundation also gave out awards. In 1930, Hughes won a Harmon Award for his first novel. It was called *Not Without Laughter*.

Financial Aid

One of Hughes's patrons was named Amy Spingarn. She was the wife of an NAACP leader. She gave Hughes $300 to pay for his Lincoln University classes.

Impressive Group

Hughes worked on *Fire!!* with writers Zora Neale Hurston, Wallace Thurman, Countee Cullen, Richard Bruce Nugent, and Aaron Douglas. These are some of the biggest names from the Harlem Renaissance.

Zora Neale Hurston

Woman's Work

Zora Neale Hurston moved to Harlem from Florida during the Great Migration. She was a writer and a friend of Langston Hughes. Hurston's ***Their Eyes Were Watching God*** was published in 1937. It is still a very popular book.

The neighborhood of Harlem in New York City

Harlem in 1927

Harlem Speaks

Hughes made a name for himself in Harlem. He wrote about the people who lived there. He wrote about their lives, their music, and their art.

Unlike many authors at that time, Hughes told stories about common working men and women. He saw the importance of their daily lives. He even wrote in the **dialect** of those ordinary people. That means that he wrote the way people spoke. Some critics did not like this. But Hughes wanted to show the real lives of African Americans.

During his years in Harlem, Hughes met other African American writers. They worked together to publish a literary magazine. They called the magazine *Fire!!* because they wanted their writing to burn up old ideas. They published only one issue, but their work inspired others.

In France, it inspired a movement. A movement is a group of people who work together to reach a common goal. French speakers with African heritage started the Negritude (NEG-ri-tood) Movement. This was a push for French-speaking blacks to celebrate their history.

Hughes's writing helped start the Negritude Movement in France.

Traveling Man

Exploring the World

Hughes felt at home in Harlem, but he still wanted to see the world. In the early 1930s, he traveled to Cuba and Haiti (HEY-tee). Hughes had long been interested in Haiti. The small island nation was the world's first independent Black **republic**. Hughes hoped to gather details to write an **opera** about Haiti's history. He spent about three months in the Caribbean (care-uh-BEE-uhn).

Hughes wanted to write an opera about the island nation of Haiti.

After returning to Harlem for a short time, Hughes went on another trip. This time, he traveled through the American South. He read his poems to schoolchildren, university students, cotton pickers, and anyone else who gathered to hear his work. He gave more than 50 poetry readings and gained many new fans.

The red star came to symbolize Communism.

Langston Hughes surrounded by young Russian writers

Next, Hughes traveled to the Soviet Union with a group of African Americans. The group was planning to make a movie about **race relations** in the United States. The project ended, but Hughes stayed in the Soviet Union. He liked what he saw there. The government provided schools and medical care for all its people. He also noticed that there was no segregation.

Communism

The Soviet Union practiced Communism. Communism is a system of government in which the state controls the economy and distributes goods equally among the people. In a Communist economy, the government controls all businesses. It also owns all the land. All land and jobs are shared equally so that no one has more than anyone else.

Capitalism

The United States practices capitalism. Capitalism allows people to own businesses. Instead of working for the government, people can work for themselves. In a capitalist country, there may be a wide gap between the rich and the poor.

Senator Joseph McCarthy

An anti-lynching banner

Looking for Traitors

Senator Joseph McCarthy was afraid Communism would come to the United States. In the early 1950s, he publicly accused many people of being Communists. The term *McCarthyism* is taken from his name. It means to accuse someone of something without any proof.

Hughes testifies before the HUAC.

Are You a Communist?

In 1953, Hughes was forced to **testify** before the House Un-American Activities Committee (HUAC). This group was formed by the House of Representatives. The group asked writers, actors, directors, musicians, and many others if they had ever been Communists. If they did not answer, they were put in jail.

Politics in Action

Travel has a way of changing people. This was true for Hughes. He came home from the Soviet Union full of new ideas. He wanted to make America a better place for African Americans.

In 1934, Hughes became president of the League of Struggle for Negro Rights. The League was started by the American Communist Party. It worked to end police cruelty, Jim Crow Laws, and **lynchings** in America. Lynching, or hanging, was a popular way for angry Southerners to take out their frustrations on freedmen.

The League also worked to end practices that were unfair to black people around the world. At that time, many European countries had **colonies** in the West Indies and Africa. A colony is land controlled by another country. The League worked to help these colonies gain independence.

Later, Hughes's association with the League complicated his life. In 1947, the United States found itself at odds with the Soviet Union. This led to an ongoing conflict between Western countries and Communist countries. It became known as the Cold War. The United States government worried about traitors. The Federal Bureau of Investigation (FBI) spied on Hughes and other suspected Communists. Hughes was labeled a "security risk" until 1959.

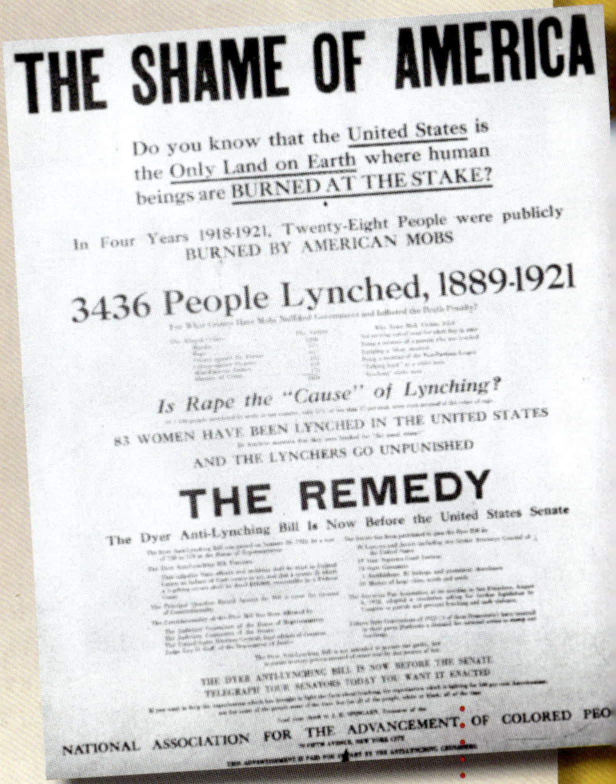

A NAACP anti-lynching poster

Hard at Work

Time to Write

By the age of 32, Hughes had published poems, essays, and a novel. After years traveling the world, he was ready to try new genres, or types, of writing. Once he was settled back in Harlem, he got right to work.

In 1934, Hughes published his first short story collection titled *The Ways of White Folks*. In 1935, he wrote a Broadway play. Next, he wrote about the Spanish Civil War.

Hughes in Harlem

In 1938, he started three theater companies and wrote plays for them. In 1940, he wrote his first autobiography, titled *The Big Sea*. In the book, Hughes wrote about the adventures of his young life. Later, he wrote a second autobiography about his adult life.

In 1942, Hughes started writing a newspaper column. He created two characters whose funny conversations dealt with important social issues. The main character was Jesse B. Semple. "Simple," as he was called, was a poor African American man in Harlem. The other character was a writer, much like Hughes. These stories made Hughes more popular than ever.

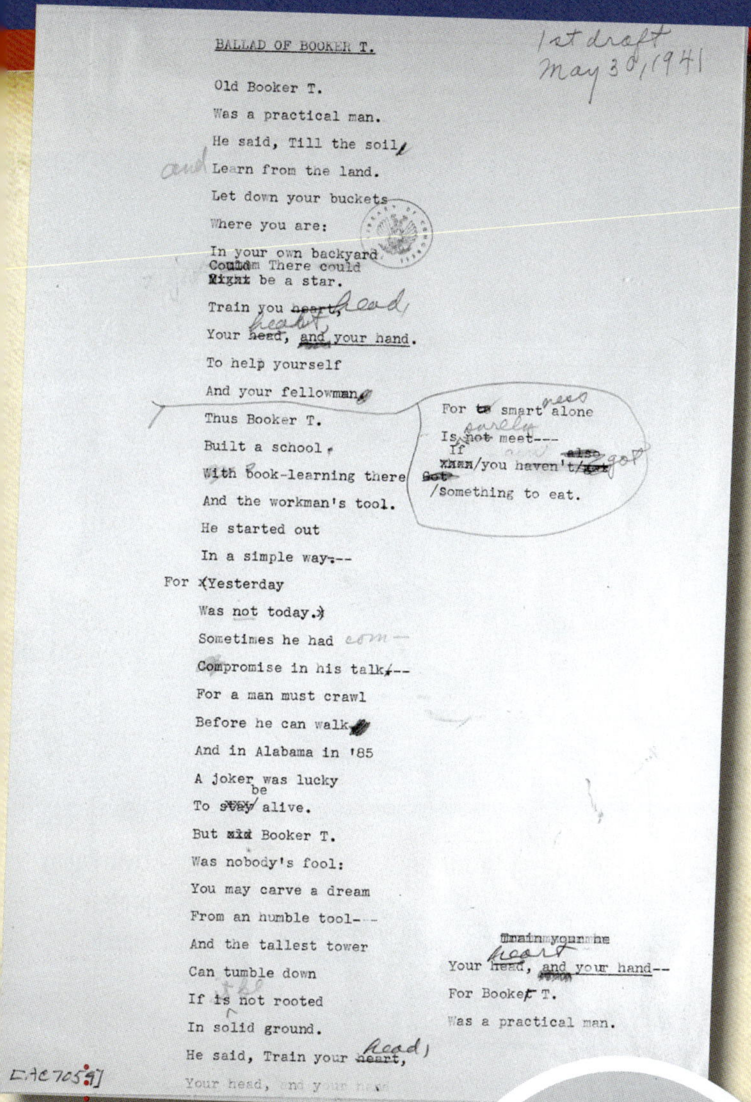
BALLAD OF BOOKER T.

1st draft May 30, 1941

Old Booker T.
Was a practical man.
He said, Till the soil,
and Learn from the land.
Let down your buckets
Where you are:
In your own backyard
Could There could
Might be a star.
Train you heart, head,
Your head, and your hand.
To help yourself
And your fellowman.

Thus Booker T.
Built a school,
With book-learning there
And the workman's tool.
He started out
In a simple way---
For Yesterday
Was not today.
Sometimes he had
Compromise in his talk---
For a man must crawl
Before he can walk.
And in Alabama in '85
A joker was lucky
To stay alive.
But Booker T.
Was nobody's fool:
You may carve a dream
From an humble tool---
And the tallest tower
Can tumble down
If it's not rooted
In solid ground.
He said, Train your heart,
Your head, and your hand

For to smart alone
Is not meet---
If man/you haven't got
Something to eat.

Train your heart
Your head, and your hand--
For Booker T.
Was a practical man.

First draft of *Ballad of Booker T.*

Booker T. Washington

A Ballad for Booker

In 1941, Hughes wrote "Ballad of Booker T." This poem was about Booker T. Washington. Washington was a slave. He was freed at the age of nine when the Civil War ended. He went on to become a college professor. Later, he started the Tuskegee Institute. It was a college for African Americans. It helped them learn practical skills, like farming. Some people criticized Washington for this. They thought African Americans should be learning more than practical skills. But Hughes admired Washington and his effort to help African Americans.

Stories for Kids

Hughes also wrote books for children. With a friend, he wrote a storybook called *Popo and Fifina*. It tells the story of two Haitian kids.

Political Opinions

After his time in the Soviet Union, Hughes became more political. This means that he was interested in the workings of government. He had new ideas about how the United States government should work. He began to write about these ideas in his poetry and essays.

Merry-Go-Round

In his poem "Merry Go Round," Hughes writes about Jim Crow Laws and segregation. He tells the story of an African American child from the South that wants to ride a merry-go-round in the North. But there is no Jim Crow section and there is no back on the merry-go-round. The child is confused and does not know where to sit. In the poem, the child asks a man, "Where's the horse/For a kid that's black?"

Civil Rights protest march

Dr. Martin Luther King Jr.

Civil Rights Movement

Hughes had been writing about the African American experience since he was a teenager. But his travels made him want to do more than write. He wanted to change hearts and minds. He began to write boldly about civil rights. Civil rights are the rights of people to have personal freedom and fair treatment under the law.

In the early 1950s, African Americans in the South started to protest segregation. This grew into the Civil Rights Movement. Dr. Martin Luther King Jr. and other leaders organized **boycotts**, marches, sit-ins, and peaceful demonstrations. Racist white Southerners fought back with violence. They bombed churches, jailed protesters, and lynched innocent people.

Northerners were outraged by the violence. They demanded that the United States government protect the rights of African Americans. Many of them joined the Civil Rights Movement.

President John F. Kennedy proposed a new civil rights bill. It took 10 years of protests, but the Civil Rights Act became law in 1964. The Civil Rights Movement succeeded! Many people say that Hughes's poetry had inspired the leaders to dream big.

President John F. Kennedy

Dreams Realized

By the end of his career, Langston Hughes was supporting himself with his writing. He was the first African American writer to achieve this level of success. He published 16 books of poetry, two novels, and three collections of short stories. He was the author of four volumes of essays, 20 plays, three autobiographies, and many magazine articles. He stretched into popular culture with a collection of children's poetry, musicals, operas, and even radio and television scripts. He had earned the title voice of the Harlem Renaissance.

Toward the end of his life, Hughes began to devote his time to helping young writers. He became a **mentor**. Two of the writers Hughes mentored were Chinua Achebe (CHIN-wah ah-CHEY-bey) and Alice Walker. Both have gone on to sell many books and win major awards.

In 1947, Hughes was finally able to buy a house in his beloved Harlem. That had been his goal since his early days. He lived in the house until his death in 1967 at the age of 65.

Hughes in 1960

Successful Student

Alice Walker was the first African American woman to win the Pulitzer Prize for fiction. She won the award for *The Color Purple*.

International Acclaim

Chinua Achebe was born in Nigeria, West Africa. He was the first West African author to become famous around the world.

Glossary

abolitionist—a person who worked to end slavery

activist—a person who takes action to change society

boycotts—refusals to deal with a company or group as a form of protest

civil rights—the rights of personal liberty guaranteed to Americans by the 13th and 14th Amendments to the Constitution and by acts of Congress

colonies—countries or areas ruled by another country

dialect—a regional way of speaking

discrimination—unfair treatment of a person or people based on race, religion, age, or other characteristics

engineer—a person who designs or builds technical machinery

freight—goods carried by commercial transportation

heritage—something possessed as a result of one's birth

historian—a person who studies or writes about history

jazz—a type of music that combines African and European sounds

jazz poetry—a type of poetry that uses the rhythm of jazz music

Jim Crow Laws—laws that kept whites and African Americans segregated

literary—relating to written works with artistic value

lynchings—hangings by mob actions, done without a fair trial

mentor—an experienced adviser

migrants—people who move to a new place to live

opera—a play that is sung with an orchestra

patrons—people who generously give others support and approval

philanthropists—people who give artists money to support their art

publisher—one that prints and sells printed materials such as books, magazines, or newspapers

race relations—the way people of different races get along in a society

renaissance—new beginning

republic—a form of government with elected representatives

segregation—laws and rules that keep the races separate

stanza—a division in a poem that forms a separate unit within the poem

testify—to make a formal statement of what one swears is true

Index

Your Turn!

After World War I, African Americans began fleeing the South in large numbers. They headed to northern cities in search of new opportunities and more freedom. Many African Americans, including the writer Langston Hughes, settled in New York City's Harlem neighborhood.

Get the Scoop!

Study the painting above of the southern train station. Imagine that you are a newspaper reporter in the South in 1917. You have been sent to this station to get the scoop on the Great Migration. Write a news story that answers the questions *Who, What, When, Where, Why,* and *How.* Include quotations from some of the travelers.